This book is dedicated
to Roussey,
an American Bulldog,
a faithful companion.

I'm so happy to meet you my tail is wagging! My name is Queen. My friends and I are going to help you adopt and care for a new pet.

Hello, young friend! I'm Henry.
There are a few things you need to know
before you welcome a new dog
into your home.

Hi, my name is Meatball.
When you
meet your dog
at the animal shelter,
be sure an adult
is with you
throughout the
introduction.
Dogs sometimes
scare easily
because we
are afraid
of being hurt.

My name is Bella. Queen asked me to
remind you to be careful around me.
Please don't suddenly take my toys,
crate, bed, or other stuff.
Please be careful when you touch me.
Slow and gentle is the rule.

Hi! My name is Canelo, and I'm here to remind you not to roughhouse with me. Please don't climb on me, yell, run, or grab me, my toys, or treats. I love it when people are quiet and kind.

My name is Pink, and I like to play. Please remember not to bother me when I'm eating. Don't take my food from me. I know you wouldn't like it if another kid took your food away from you. You'd be angry, and just like you, I'd be angry too.

Hello there! My name is Sparky. My best buddy Queen said this is one of the most important rules you should know. NEVER put your face in a dog's face, because some animals do that when they want to fight. So, if we're going to be friends, you'll want to treat me gently, and don't get close to my face.

Hi again, it's Queen with another important reminder. Please be careful when you pet me. Not all dogs like to be touched on top of the head.

So, what should you do?

Pet me gently on the neck.

If I don't like it,

try another time.

Meeko here with two pieces of advice. One, never leave a dog in a hot car. If the air conditioning isn't on and it's a hot day, please take me with you! Two, don't tie me up outside alone. This can make me cranky and sick.

Meatball
Meeko
Sparky
Queen
Henry
Canelo
Pink

You'll find dogs like us at your local animal shelter. Ask your parents if they'll bring you to meet us soon! We're ready to go home with you if you promise to be gentle, kind, and see that we always have food and fresh water. We like a lot of affection (and sometimes a belly rub too)!

Bella

This book is made
possible with the
help of the staff and
many volunteers at
Gulf Coast
Humane Society
in Fort Myers, Florida,
established in 1947.

Every pet deserves
a loving home.

Please visit

gulfcoasthumanesociety.org

Illustrations

by

Jo Bro

Made in the USA
Middletown, DE
10 March 2024

51075604R00015